Plant Name   **Date**

Water
Requirements 💧   💧💧   💧💧💧   Sunlight ☀ ☀ ●

☐ Seed   ☐ Transplant

Date	Event

Notes

Outcome

Uses

Purchased at: _____   Price: _____

Plant Name

Date Planted

Water Requirements 🫧　🫧🫧　🫧🫧🫧

Sunlight ☀ ◐ ●

☐ Seed　　☐ Transplant

Date	Event

Notes

Outcome

Uses

Purchased at: _____　　Price: _____

Plant Name   **Date Planted**

Water
Requirements   💧   💧💧   💧💧💧   Sunlight   ☀ ◐ ●

☐ Seed   ☐ Transplant

Date	Event

Notes

Outcome

Uses

Purchased at: _____   Price: _____

Plant Name   **Date Planted**

Water
Requirements   💧   💧💧   💧💧💧   Sunlight   ☀ ☀ ●

☐ Seed   ☐ Transplant

Date	Event

Notes

Outcome

Uses

Purchased at: _____   Price: _____

Plant Name   **Date Planted**

Water
Requirements   💧   💧💧   💧💧💧   Sunlight   ☀ ◑ ●

☐ Seed   ☐ Transplant

Date	Event

Notes

Outcome

Uses

Purchased at: _____   Price: _____

Plant Name   **Date Planted**

Water
Requirements   💧   💧💧   💧💧💧   Sunlight   ☀   ◐   ●

☐ Seed   ☐ Transplant

Date	Event

Notes

Outcome

Uses

Purchased at: _____   Price: _____

Plant Name   **Date Planted**

Water
Requirements   💧   💧💧   💧💧💧   Sunlight   ☀   ◐   ●

☐ Seed   ☐ Transplant

Date	Event

Notes

Outcome

Uses

Purchased at: _____   Price: _____

Plant Name   **Date Planted**

Water
Requirements   💧   💧💧   💧💧💧   Sunlight   ☼ ◐ ●

☐ Seed   ☐ Transplant

Date	Event

Notes

Outcome

Uses

Purchased at: _____   Price: _____

Plant Name   **Date Planted**

Water
Requirements   💧   💧💧   💧💧💧   Sunlight   ☀ ☀ ⬤

☐ Seed   ☐ Transplant

Date	Event

Notes

Outcome

Uses

Purchased at: _____   Price: _____

Plant Name   **Date Planted**

Water
Requirements   💧   💧💧   💧💧💧   Sunlight   ☀ ☀ ⚫

☐ Seed   ☐ Transplant

Date	Event

Notes

Outcome

Uses

Purchased at: _____   Price: _____

Plant Name   **Date Planted**

Water
Requirements   🌢 🌢🌢 🌢🌢🌢   Sunlight   ☀ ◑ ●

☐ Seed   ☐ Transplant

Date	Event

Notes

Outcome

Uses

Purchased at: _____   Price: _____

Plant Name

Date Planted

Water
Requirements 💧 💧💧 💧💧💧

Sunlight ☀ ☀ ⬤

☐ Seed   ☐ Transplant

Date	Event

Notes

Outcome

Uses

Purchased at: _____   Price: _____

Plant Name   **Date Planted**

Water
Requirements   💧   💧💧   💧💧💧

Sunlight   ☀ ☀ ●

☐ Seed   ☐ Transplant

Date	Event

Notes

Outcome

Uses

Purchased at: _____   Price: _____

Plant Name   **Date Planted**

Water
Requirements   💧   💧💧   💧💧💧   Sunlight   ☼   ◑   ●

☐ Seed   ☐ Transplant

Date	Event

Notes

Outcome

Uses

Purchased at: _____   Price: _____

Plant Name   **Date Planted**

Water
Requirements 🌢 🌢🌢 🌢🌢🌢   Sunlight ☀ ☀ ⬤

☐ Seed   ☐ Transplant

Date	Event

Notes

Outcome

Uses

Purchased at: _____   Price: _____

Plant Name   **Date Planted**

Water Requirements   💧   💧💧   💧💧💧   Sunlight ☀ ◐ ●

☐ Seed   ☐ Transplant

Date	Event

Notes

Outcome

Uses

Purchased at: _____   Price: _____

Plant Name   **Date Planted**

Water
Requirements   💧   💧💧   💧💧💧   Sunlight   ☀ ☀ ⬤

☐ Seed   ☐ Transplant

Date	Event

Notes

Outcome

Uses

Purchased at: _____   Price: _____

Plant Name

Date Planted

Water
Requirements 💧 💧💧 💧💧💧

Sunlight ☀ ◐ ⬤

☐ Seed   ☐ Transplant

Date	Event

Notes

Outcome

Uses

Purchased at: _____   Price: _____

Plant Name   **Date Planted**

Water
Requirements   🌢 🌢🌢 🌢🌢🌢   Sunlight   ☀ ◑ ●

☐ Seed   ☐ Transplant

Date	Event

Notes

Outcome

Uses

Purchased at: _____   Price: _____

Plant Name   **Date Planted**

Water
Requirements 💧   💧💧   💧💧💧   Sunlight   ☀ ☀ ⬤

☐ Seed   ☐ Transplant

Date	Event

Notes

Outcome

Uses

Purchased at: _____   Price: _____

Plant Name   **Date Planted**

Water
Requirements 💧 💧💧 💧💧💧   Sunlight ☀ ◐ ●

☐ Seed   ☐ Transplant

Date	Event

Notes

Outcome

Uses

Purchased at: _____   Price: _____

Plant Name   **Date Planted**

Water
Requirements 💧   💧💧   💧💧💧   Sunlight   ☀ ☀ ●

☐ Seed   ☐ Transplant

Date	Event

Notes

Outcome

Uses

Purchased at: _____   Price: _____

Plant Name

Date Planted

Water
Requirements

Sunlight

☐ Seed   ☐ Transplant

Date	Event

Notes

Outcome

Uses

Purchased at: _____   Price: _____

Plant Name   **Date Planted**

Water
Requirements ⬤ ⬤⬤ ⬤⬤⬤   Sunlight ☀ ☀ ⬤

☐ Seed   ☐ Transplant

Date	Event

Notes

Outcome

Uses

Purchased at: _____   Price: _____

Plant Name

Date Planted

Water
Requirements 💧 💧💧 💧💧💧

Sunlight ☀ ◐ ●

☐ Seed   ☐ Transplant

Date	Event

Notes

Outcome

Uses

Purchased at: _____   Price: _____

Plant Name   **Date Planted**

Water
Requirements   🌢 🌢🌢 🌢🌢🌢   Sunlight ☀ ☼ ●

☐ Seed   ☐ Transplant

Date	Event

Notes

Outcome

Uses

Purchased at: _____   Price: _____

Plant Name   **Date Planted**

Water
Requirements   💧   💧💧   💧💧💧   Sunlight   ☀ ☀ ●

☐ Seed   ☐ Transplant

Date	Event

Notes

Outcome

Uses

Purchased at: _____   Price: _____

Plant Name   **Date Planted**

Water
Requirements 🌢   🌢🌢   🌢🌢🌢   Sunlight ☀ ☼ ⬤

☐ Seed   ☐ Transplant

Date	Event

Notes

Outcome

Uses

Purchased at: _____   Price: _____

Plant Name   **Date Planted**

Water
Requirements   💧   💧💧   💧💧💧   Sunlight   ☀   ◐   ●

☐ Seed   ☐ Transplant

Date	Event

Notes

Outcome

Uses

Purchased at: _____   Price: _____

Plant Name   **Date Planted**

Water
Requirements   💧   💧💧   💧💧💧   Sunlight   ☀ ☀ ●

☐ Seed   ☐ Transplant

Date	Event

Notes

Outcome

Uses

Purchased at: _____   Price: _____

Plant Name

Date Planted

Water
Requirements 💧 💧💧 💧💧💧

Sunlight ☀ ◑ ●

☐ Seed ☐ Transplant

Date	Event

Notes

Outcome

Uses

Purchased at: _____ Price: _____

Plant Name

Date Planted

Water
Requirements 💧 💧💧 💧💧💧

Sunlight ☀ ☀ ●

☐ Seed   ☐ Transplant

Date	Event

Notes

Outcome

Uses

Purchased at: _____   Price: _____

Plant Name

Date Planted

Water
Requirements

Sunlight

☐ Seed   ☐ Transplant

Date	Event

Notes

Outcome

Uses

Purchased at: _____   Price: _____

Plant Name   **Date Planted**

Water
Requirements   💧   💧💧   💧💧💧   Sunlight   ☀ ☀ ●

☐ Seed   ☐ Transplant

Date	Event

Notes

Outcome

Uses

Purchased at: _____   Price: _____

Plant Name

Date Planted

Water Requirements 💧 💧💧 💧💧💧

Sunlight ☀ ☼ ●

☐ Seed   ☐ Transplant

Date	Event

Notes

Outcome

Uses

Purchased at: _____   Price: _____

Plant Name   **Date Planted**

Water
Requirements   💧   💧💧   💧💧💧   Sunlight   ☀ ☀ ⬤

☐ Seed   ☐ Transplant

Date	Event

Notes

Outcome

Uses

Purchased at: _____   Price: _____

Plant Name   **Date Planted**

Water
Requirements   💧   💧💧   💧💧💧   Sunlight   ☀ ☀ ●

☐ Seed   ☐ Transplant

Date	Event

Notes

Outcome

Uses

Purchased at: _____   Price: _____

Plant Name   **Date Planted**

Water
Requirements   ⬤   ⬤⬤   ⬤⬤⬤   Sunlight   ☀ ◐ ⬤

☐ Seed   ☐ Transplant

Date	Event

Notes

Outcome

Uses

Purchased at: _____   Price: _____

Plant Name   **Date Planted**

Water
Requirements   💧   💧💧   💧💧💧

Sunlight   ☼   ◐   ●

☐ Seed   ☐ Transplant

Date	Event

Notes

Outcome

Uses

Purchased at: _____   Price: _____

Plant Name   **Date Planted**

Water
Requirements   💧 💧💧 💧💧💧   Sunlight ☀ ◐ ●

☐ Seed   ☐ Transplant

Date	Event

Notes

Outcome

Uses

Purchased at: _____   Price: _____

Plant Name

Date Planted

Water
Requirements   💧   💧💧   💧💧💧

Sunlight   ☀ ◐ ●

☐ Seed   ☐ Transplant

Date	Event

Notes

Outcome

Uses

Purchased at: _____   Price: _____

Plant Name   **Date Planted**

Water
Requirements   🌢 🌢🌢 🌢🌢🌢   Sunlight   ☀ ◐ ●

☐ Seed   ☐ Transplant

Date	Event

Notes

Outcome

Uses

Purchased at: _____   Price: _____

Plant Name   **Date Planted**

Water
Requirements   💧   💧💧   💧💧💧   Sunlight   ☀ ☀ ⬤

☐ Seed   ☐ Transplant

Date	Event

Notes

Outcome

Uses

Purchased at: _____   Price: _____

Plant Name   **Date Planted**

Water
Requirements   💧   💧💧   💧💧💧   Sunlight   ☀ ☀ ⬤

☐ Seed   ☐ Transplant

Date	Event

Notes

Outcome

Uses

Purchased at: _____   Price: _____

Plant Name   **Date Planted**

Water
Requirements   💧 💧💧 💧💧💧   Sunlight ☀ ☀ ●

☐ Seed   ☐ Transplant

Date	Event

Notes

Outcome

Uses

Purchased at: _____   Price: _____

Plant Name   **Date Planted**

Water
Requirements   💧   💧💧   💧💧💧   Sunlight   ☀   ◐   ●

☐ Seed   ☐ Transplant

Date	Event

Notes

Outcome

Uses

Purchased at: _____   Price: _____

Plant Name   **Date Planted**

Water
Requirements   💧   💧💧   💧💧💧   Sunlight   ☀   🌤   ●

☐ Seed   ☐ Transplant

Date	Event

Notes

Outcome

Uses

Purchased at: _____   Price: _____

Plant Name   **Date Planted**

Water
Requirements   💧   💧💧   💧💧💧   Sunlight   ☀ ☀ ⬤

☐ Seed   ☐ Transplant

Date	Event

Notes

Outcome

Uses

Purchased at: _____   Price: _____

Plant Name   **Date Planted**

Water
Requirements   💧 💧💧 💧💧💧   Sunlight ☀ ☀ ⬤

☐ Seed   ☐ Transplant

Date	Event

Notes

Outcome

Uses

Purchased at: _____   Price: _____

Plant Name   **Date Planted**

Water
Requirements   🌢   🌢🌢   🌢🌢🌢   Sunlight   ☀ ◐ ●

☐ Seed   ☐ Transplant

Date	Event

Notes

Outcome

Uses

Purchased at: _____   Price: _____

Plant Name   **Date Planted**

Water
Requirements   💧   💧💧   💧💧💧   Sunlight   ☀ ☀ ●

☐ Seed   ☐ Transplant

Date	Event

Notes

Outcome

Uses

Purchased at: _____   Price: _____

Plant Name   **Date Planted**

Water
Requirements 💧   💧💧   💧💧💧

Sunlight ☀ ☀ ●

☐ Seed   ☐ Transplant

Date	Event

Notes

Outcome

Uses

Purchased at: _____   Price: _____

Plant Name   **Date Planted**

Water
Requirements   🌢   🌢🌢   🌢🌢🌢   Sunlight   ☼   ◐   ●

☐ Seed   ☐ Transplant

Date	Event

Notes

Outcome

Uses

Purchased at: _____   Price: _____

Plant Name   **Date Planted**

Water
Requirements   💧   💧💧   💧💧💧   Sunlight   ☀ ◐ ●

☐ Seed   ☐ Transplant

Date	Event

Notes

Outcome

Uses

Purchased at: _____   Price: _____

Plant Name

Date Planted

Water Requirements 💧 💧💧 💧💧💧

Sunlight ☀ ◐ ●

☐ Seed   ☐ Transplant

Date	Event

Notes

Outcome

Uses

Purchased at: _____   Price: _____

Plant Name   **Date Planted**

Water
Requirements   💧   💧💧   💧💧💧   Sunlight   ☀ ☀ ●

☐ Seed   ☐ Transplant

Date	Event

Notes

Outcome

Uses

Purchased at: _____   Price: _____

Plant Name   **Date Planted**

Water
Requirements   💧 💧💧 💧💧💧 💧💧💧💧   Sunlight   ☀ ◑ ●

☐ Seed   ☐ Transplant

Date	Event

Notes

Outcome

Uses

Purchased at: _____   Price: _____

Plant Name   **Date Planted**

Water
Requirements   💧   💧💧   💧💧💧   Sunlight   ☀ ☀ ●

☐ Seed   ☐ Transplant

Date	Event

Notes

Outcome

Uses

Purchased at: _____   Price: _____

Plant Name

Date Planted

Water
Requirements

Sunlight

☐ Seed

☐ Transplant

Date	Event

Notes

Outcome

Uses

Purchased at: _____

Price: _____

Plant Name   **Date Planted**

Water
Requirements   💧   💧💧   💧💧💧   Sunlight   ☀ ☀ ●

☐ Seed   ☐ Transplant

Date	Event

Notes

Outcome

Uses

Purchased at: _____   Price: _____